FOREWORD

Mentoring Startup Entrepreneurs Part V

By now our Startup Entrepreneur - (we shall rename them Startup Entrepreneurs as Startpreneur) would have decided to structure business and obtained one of the following Legal status by registering their company as:

1. One Person Company

2. Private Limited Company

3. Limited Liability Partnership

4. Public Limited Company or

5. Section 8 NGO company.

You may have also taken steps to Secure your business by obtaining necessary

- Trademark Registration
- Sent replies to trademark objections
- Renewed your Trademark
- Licensing your Trademark
- Copyrighted your Registration and/or
- Replied to Copyright objections

Things I suppose Startpreneurs may have already completed or may be in the process.

1. You may have also familiarized yourself with the ROC return filing, Appointment of Directions, their Resignations, Change of Office Address, increasing capital of the company as also the closure procedures involved (just in case) for OPC, LLP, Pvt.Ltd.

2. Depending upon what you Sell - Products/ Services or Productized Services you may also be thinking about the Quality aspects and ISO certification etc.

3. You may have also familiarized yourself with the Startup India Scheme.

4. You may have also looked up various Apps which give options like Mudra Bank, Bank Loan schemes.

5. Maybe, someone from their experience would have also spoken to you about Venture Capital, Private Equity, Angel Investing etc. about which you may be in the mode to gather more information or learn from other Mentors/ Specialists.

6. You may even be attending some of the FinTech or other Startup related programs organized by different Industry Associations/ Institutes/ Universities / others.

DEDICATION

Getting Started

In this Part V, we shall discuss several Business Ideas, Projects and I shall share with your Real-life experiences of Startpreneurs who came in touch with me over the years. These experiences may help the readers - Startups, Entrepreneurs or aspirants of starting business, people facing some mid-career crisis like retrenchment, loss of job and may be wanting to enter the BOOM - Being One's Own Man - Startpreneur phase of their life with some apprehensions about the likelihood of success, Risks involved, financial worries, uncertainties etc.

In the Real-Life experiences that I shall share many of them will be narrated from a Startpreneurs' point of view. It is my observation that Male or Female, Startpreneurs have Alpha personality traits and it is the ability of the Mentor to bring out the Lions within them.

This Series is dedicated to my several Ex-colleagues many of whom turned Startpreneurs. To my wife, Madhura Parkhe for inspiring me to write the book and sharing her Oil Paintings as Cover Pages for some of my books.

My special thanks are due to my several Personal, Official, Spiritual Mentors and many friends who kept motivating me to write a book someday. Due to space constraint, I am unable to name them all yet I express my sincere gratitude to them.

My special gratitude is due to my Executive Coaching Gurus Late Thomas J. Leonard of CoachVille and Dr. Marshall Goldsmith whose inspiration is most invaluable and no words of thanks and gratitude will be enough to express my feelings towards them.

Finally, to KDP Amazon, Createspace, Draft2Digital without whose support this would see the light of the day. Thank you all.

COPYRIGHT

© Dhananjaya Parkhe - ALL RIGHTS RESERVED.

CHAPTER 1

What is an Alpha Personality?

How do Startpreneurs display them.

Let us first understand the traits of an Alpha male and Alpha female first.

How your Alpha personality type will give you an advantage in your business and life and how you can become successful by channeling your alpha traits as a Startpreneur is where a seasoned Mentor as a good judge of People helps you.

Who can be called an Alpha Male?
Alpha male can be described as Mr. Popularity. He leads life as the leader of the pack. Takes the lead in organizing Office parties, constantly determining the best way for the team to get those long-term projects done. You are outgoing. These roles you seem to always fall into are natural predilections of your alpha personality. Alpha males find it easy to take charge in multiple situations because they are always outgoing. To them, choosing an office party locale are not different than when they are needed to pick the hotel where their little team can celebrate after the team has won an Award, a game together. They are programmed for success. They are enterprising people who are destined for a life of achievements and fulfillment. Sometimes though their charm and charisma stops working wonders and they may need to reset or tune-in their machismo meter to 'just right' to reap lifetime of rewards.

The Alpha Female?
Alpha Female is Miss Confidence, who dominates an entire office full of women? They would surely have a past of rising to their college's sorority's who's who list. Their alpha personality makes them lead and be at the apex of nearly every social circle where you befriend people. The competitive spirit, ambition, can-do attitude is no less than their male counterparts. They excel in every task designated, they are aware of potential setbacks that may come to others because of your Alpha personality. They need to be cautious to know that they may not be the boss in every situation. Just a bit of relaxation may with them a promotion and a lifetime of financial security. They need to display to seniors that they are nurturing, caring and understanding of their team and therefore capable of handling management positions. They are generally misunderstood about this aspect of their traits.

Mr. Popularity and Miss Confidence. the only question should be how do you channel your alpha personality traits to take control of your life and continue to be hugely successful. In knowing those personality traits of yours that help you achieve success and those that others may be slightly turned off by, you are miles ahead of your alpha competitors.

In my Mentoring experience, I have could successfully channelize the Alpha traits into success for C-Level Executives and what I term as Startpreneurs - those who start their businesses and become successful Entrepreneurs in life.

"Those who mind don't matter, and those who matter don't mind." — Bernard M. Baruch

CHAPTER 2

Popular Startpreneur

The Popular Startpreneur

I have an ex-colleague, who is very popular - both among gentlemen as much as the ladies at the workplace. He would take lead in organizing parties - many of them at his own 3 storied house with many rooms and halls and fully decked Kitchen where he (a Hotel management graduate and ex F&B Manager) he would love to cook for them or serve a Barbeque on the terrace with drinks. Of course, music, dance were constants.

Few years later he decided to quit the job/ company and start a business of his own. He took a partner - a small office and went about getting customers as Express Aggregator. He began tasting success. He followed the same formula of popularity with his junior most staff attending his parties/ picnics at every Milestone achieved, every business success achieved. It became a very well-knit team as he had adjusted his Machismo Meter and did not feel 'low' in mingling with juniors "minions' and employees freely.

Over the years the apprehensive family, friends and colleagues began liking him do so, he could expect that they will hope for his success as much as he does. It is as if he had his own personal cheering team and when things were not going his way, he could expect these people to come in quick and help.

He acquired a partner in travel business and with him travelled the world and met several tour operators, hotels, group bookings organizers in different countries and he was hugely popular as he would invite them home for self-cooked dishes of their choice - giving the Indian hospitality a very personal touch. Not just popular - his business flourished.

His first partner introduced him to a guy who wanted a partner in his fast food Chinese cuisine business. This colleague of mine had invested in a shop in a Mall and they began operating from there. My friend did not focus on being the Chef but looked after the Purchase end which was to buy quality vegetables, poultry and meat. The business took off. However, he could not spend enough time daily going to the market and buying stuff and delegated to the two other partners. Few months later, he intervened to find cooked books, siphoning and a bad business which was making huge loss. He just took a call and closed the shop, broke off the partnership. The Alpha Male, when provoked takes charge and controls in his own hands and then won't take any opposition to his judgements and plans. In this case, the decision proved right and as a Single owner of his Express business he is still very popular among his stakeholders - Customers and Staff. A prudent businessman - he realized that he would grow business only to the extent he can self-manage and he is hugely successful and happy.

"No one can make you feel inferior without your consent." — Eleanor Roosevelt

CHAPTER 3

Leader Startpreneur

Leading is a Startpreneur trait

The Alpha has a Leadership trait. They lead by example, they take charge, like to be in a Command situation. People follow others with alpha personalities. Because others are following lead, Startpreneurs work harder to contribute to your success knowing that their own success is dependent on them and their plans.

In school / college and University days, I represented them in most Indoor/ Outdoor games and in many of them as Captain. My favorite was of course, Cricket. In school days, I once joined a local club and realized that I could start a small club of my own and enter local championships with my friends as players and team mates. Our home finances were not good. A Single parent mom was a teacher and private tutor and I was working as part-time salesman in my free time/ holidays. I also was lucky to get Government Free ship (from school fees which were discounted), Merit cum poverty scholarships and Merit scholarships. To start a club this would barely fund the need and the teammates were also from poor or middle class families.

We found a way. Call it Indian Jugaad but we realized that the Businessmen in my hometown were benevolent and were not averse to give small donations for a worthy cause. All we needed in early 70's was about INR 250 for the kit and about INR 50 as entry fee for each Championship. The later was possible to raise thru subscription from our 20 odd player members. We began practicing at a friend's bungalow where there was a Cement pitch and he was good enough to give us a Mat to cover half the pitch and a net behind. We played a tournament and reached unto Quarter finals and lost. We played few more winning some/ losing some and by year end one an important championship.

In each team, we have performers and average players and a team needs all kinds. I realized after winning that My Best Batsman team mate and Best Bowler were uneasy and I heard rumors that they wanted captaincy while majority of the team members were with me. I called them both separately for a one on one chat and said they can have the Club and build a team. I shall announce the decision, form another club and those team mates who wished to play with them would be free to go with them. They were pleasantly surprised. I left the club to them both as they patched up and agreed to run the club. Out of 20 I still had 15 team members willing to follow me. I formed another club. Continued practice. Invited some senior players for giving us some tips and entered competitions again. Our donors were happy to donate more this time as we had won a championship. Couple of these traders offered Free sandwiches, Water, in return for some publicity banners which we would put up behind out benches. Team uniforms were not in vogue - we were to use our own white pants and shirts. We played better and won 3 championships and were finalists in 3 more. I saw the same issue again. While I was the best bowler - the Best all-rounder cum Opening batsman who played, the best was bitten by the Leadership bug. I followed the same ritual and gave him my club. This time he gathered more moss and my new team was depleted by 50%. I again formed another club. Went to the donors who were magnificent. Couple of them wanted their sons to be included in our team- we were more than happy to accommodate and train them. They voluntarily gave us Cricket shoes, apart from Individual kits, Bats, Caps - Rich donors are always best.

Next year, we won all the 6 championships and this time when the similar ego issues appeared - I disbanded the club but as I was entering college, decided not to form another. Call it eccentric behavior, call me maverick but I felt and knew I can LEAD and create something out of nothing. I could manage a team well and keep most of my team together. I also learnt that I cannot have control over others' egos and "WHY PEOPLE BEHAVE THE WAY THEY DO".

Along the way, I learnt some Startpreneur lessons. For the right persuasion and a winning team - there will be backers - even if they have nothing to earn from it. Today, I mentor NGOs and the jargon used is "SOCIAL ENTREPRENEURSHIP." I also learnt that people would be willing to fund you again and again but some donors may begin looking for some 'Quid Pro Quo' and for that they would be willing to fund you even more. Being open to suggestion, receptive and accommodative to the small demands of the Funders / donors only increases your goodwill and people trust you even move.

While my psychology specialist and HR Specialist friends did not like when I gave this example at the workplace and said this trait could prove a CLM - Career Limiting Move - I couldn't care more! Frankly, I kept building team's whichever responsibility I was given in the career. It helped.

"Do not fear to be eccentric in opinion, for every opinion now accepted was once eccentric." — Bertrand Russell

CHAPTER 4

Enterprising Startpreneur

Every Penny Saved is Money Earned!
You are Enterprising"

Many of us since our childhood may be people that have sought solutions to any problems that arise. We may have practiced this skill so often all problems that you may run into appear simple."

As a Startpreneur we learn to eliminate Non-Value Added Activities from our Startup. We learn to "ÇUT' and as the famous saying goes "Applying Occam's Razor or to cut the Crap! A No-Nonsense approach" gets embedded in our actions. A Startpreneur is Enterprising and is unafraid to take ruthless decisions without any emotions.

Whether in Recession or during boom, good businesses sharpen their competitive edge by applying Lean Management principles to cost reduction., the elimination of non-value-added activities or waste in the value stream processes.

<u>Being Lean - In the Lean Management philosophy is where all activities in an organization are grouped into two categories:</u>

- value-added (VA) activities, and
- non-value-added (NVA) activities.

In Lean Management, we view, VA and NVA activities from customer's perspective. VA activities are those that bring additional value to products or services e.g. entering orders, ordering materials, laying foundations, creating codes, assembling parts and shipping of goods to customers. Customers pay for these improvements that can change the form, fit or function of a product or service. NVA activities are tasks that do not increase market form or function e.g. filing, copying, recording, waiting, counting, checking, inspecting, testing, reviewing and obtaining approvals. These activities are eliminated, simplified or reduced.

By tackling wastes from an end-to-end business process, not only can our company improve the value of its products and services, we can also achieve significant cost reduction, strengthen cash flow and emerge from the downturn with a stronger and more competitive profile.

<u>There are 7 Sources of Waste in a manufacturing environment.</u>

The explanations and examples provided below may be more relevant to manufacturing industries, the concepts can be universally applied to service industries as well.

The seven sources of waste are:

1. Waiting
2. Over-process
3. Defects
4. Excess motion
5. Transportation
6. Over-production
7. Excess inventory

1. Waiting - Idle time resulting from waiting for materials and information, e-mail queues from customers, delayed shipments, equipment or system downtime and so on.

2. Over-process - This results from unnecessary procedures due to undefined customer requirements, lack of effective communication, product changes without process changes, redundant approvals, making extra copies and excessive reporting.

3. Defects- These are errors, scrap, rework, replacements, re-inspection and re-testing. The causes are incorrect data entries, poor quality, weak process

control, inadequate training, deficient planned maintenance and customer needs that were not understood.

4. Excess motion- This refers to any movement of people or machines that does not add value to the product or service. Common causes are poor plant or office layout, double handling, inconsistent work methods and poor workplace organization.

5. Transportation- This refers to the transporting of parts, materials and files or documents around the plant or office. The causes are poor plant or office layout, widely spaced equipment and workstations, and poor understanding of the process flow.

6. Over-production- This happens when you make too much, too early and faster than is required by the next process. The causes include unclear goals, excessive lead times and outdated forecasts. Tip: You should reduce your batch size to match the rate of demand. Produce exactly to customer demand, not more.

7. Excess inventory- This happens when you have more inventory than is needed for a job. It is important to tackle excess inventory as it has a huge impact on cash flow. Tip: Review your materials purchasing strategy — where can you buy them at a cheaper price, in smaller amounts and have them delivered to you more frequently?

Eliminating Waste

The ability to identify waste in your organization is the first step towards its elimination. A common problem-solving technique is the PDCA (Plan-Do-Check-Act) approach. Involve your employees in problem-solving or process improvement. Setting a Continuous Process

For waste elimination to be successful and sustainable, an organization's senior executives need to adopt a mindset that cutting waste to cut costs is an on-going journey of continuous improvement. It should be a collaborative effort between management and employees. A common mistake for Startpreneur is to avoid is to treat waste elimination as another one-off "tool" or quick fix. It is essential to manage waste elimination as a strategic change initiative that is aligned to the organization's vision, encompassing both cultural and process transformations.

I mentioned elsewhere in this series that Making Profit in Purchase and Profit in Sales are critical for Startpreneur - Saving by eliminating waste ruthlessly is something which if the Startpreneur does not already have - a mentor can help him/ her to learn.

"Man often becomes what he believes himself to be. If I keep on saying to myself that I cannot do a certain thing, it is possible that I may end by becoming incapable of doing it. On the contrary, if I have the belief that I can do it, I shall surely acquire the capacity to do it even if I may not have it at the beginning." — Mohandas Karamchand Gandhi.

CHAPTER 5

Charming & Charismatic

Wonderful Startpreneurs'- Alpha Male/ Female trait

Not all Startpreneurs Possess Charm and Charisma and not all of them are diplomatic - some firmly believe in calling "a spade a spade".

Part of being successful relies on our ability to share your success and the rewards of it with others. People want to be a part of your success because we are just so appealing, warm and welcoming.

This exchange of a would be Startreneur with his boss after putting in his papers is quite interesting: First the Employee is narrating his story.

"Do you want to know why I was unable to start on my own for several years" and "I kept thinking of starting my own business. But each time when it came to resigning I always had a fear that I would lose everything I have, if I failed. "And "I finally decided to resign. Post resignation

My Boss naturally asked me "Do you have another offer in hand?".

When I told, him I had none and planned to start my business, he made fun of me and said

"I did not know that you are such a fool, you want to leave such a great career to struggle all your life?".

He further added "The probability of success is only 1% and the probability to return to a Corporate role after being a failed entrepreneur is Zero!".

He then asked me was I such a dare devil that I was not afraid of failure?

I said I was, and I would like to still give it a try!

He asked whether I had a business plan/idea and I said I had none. I just knew I had to start something and about that I was clear.

He asked if I have a fallback cushion with a rich supporting family or in—laws? And what is my plan B, I had to admit, I had none! :)

Finally, when he knew his probing questions are neither dissuading me or not interesting me, he confessed, -"I always desired to be on my own but lacked courage. The risk for me is too large and I just sincerely wish that you succeed."

Here is another anecdote: This one is a Post on Social media.

"If you are scared to lose what you have? If fear is stopping, you? I am Looking for b2b sales folks pan country across levels. People with (0-15 yrs. exp) for my business"- Like or comment with your email."

The opening itself told me that that this was a success story. Someone who was determined to 'Rough it out" and see for himself what wars he must fight to survive. Apparently, the writer has survived and doing well and Hiring!

I am sharing this as I found a naive charm in the writer and truthfulness and as it closely resembled with my own story where I Failed after three years of entrepreneurship and was lucky to land a job in a MNC as my Plan B, C, D thru unto Z had failed and I was looking at bankruptcy in the face. But I was similarly naive, charming and truthful. I still had some charisma left which helped me with the interview preparation and Honesty helped.

Many of the Executives in a mid-career crisis begin to face the BOOM stage willy-nilly as no one is willing to push their CV for a senior / FAT salaried jobs mad due to their lifestyle they are unable to adjust to any lower income jobs. As C-Suite Mentor I have helped some in getting jobs but mostly I have motivated them to be Startpreneurs like this case I mentioned.

When we begin to look within for Strengths rather than focusing on weaknesses which others point out and "Trying to become strongest in our Weakest spots" I have helped people find their Real strength and Capitalize it as it is my firm belief that we can only capitalize out Strength/s NOT weaknesses.

Charm and Charisma in an individual is one of the strengths which helps in not only marketing their products. Services or their company but also their own personal image and reputation enhancement.

"When someone tells me "no," it doesn't mean I can't do it, it simply means I can't do it with them." – Karen E. Quinones Miller

CHAPTER 6

Confidence thy name is Startpreneur

Great trait: Confidence and Courage.

The Confident Startpreneur

New opportunities are constantly presenting themselves and we have enough confidence to make ourselves available for all of them.

1. One of my friends to whom I provided Pro-Bono Mentor advice was an experienced Director of a Business school. He was starting a new business school of a different kind. It was to serve primarily the interests of one large booming semi-organized sector in India where there was potential as per his market research for not just placing MBAs but also people who could be skilled in other aspects of business with theory and practical skills training.

2. As a Pert Ii We found some international tie-ups with European Institutes to provide Executive MBA programs as also normal MBA programs with International faculty coming to India for a Semester and a Study visit program for the students abroad for a fortnight.

3. We also looked at and as Part III tied up with a University which had an outreach program by meeting all their requirements, terms, conditions, Quality aspects and security from an examination center perspective

4. The part iv of his business plan was to have an Executive Development Program with the help of management experts/ friendly professors as faculty in the neighborhood Industrial estates and corporate houses for training their mid-level managers. One sub-set of this plan was to build and we did build a

small team with a mission to provide HR on-boarding process services to corporates right from recruitment to induction, on the job training and final job placement.

5. A tie-up with the Skills development Council of the Industry was done, several entry level jobs selected, training curriculum and certification process and training hours were agreed. The program was funded by the Government of indicate had backers, private funders and partners. He had invested what best he could, providing some emergency funds with wife for an Exit day. Many people taunted him, criticizes him.

6. We invited reputed people from Industry to join Academic Council, Advisory Board and as patrons.

The initial response form the sector / industry was fabulous and people were discussing and agreeing MOUs, and some large Universities opened competing MBA courses in the same discipline.

Executive Development Program and HR On-boarding business took off well. International tie-up was fledgling due to non-competitive pricing and perceived benefit lacunae but the flagship program wasn't just taking off. The breakeven was 60 student's intakes per year which did not get achieved for 5 full years. In the interim, many full time and part time faculty, staff members joined and were doing their bit for business development.

My advisory was formally for a 3-month duration and later I would call him as a friend or met him twice in his office as a courtesy. He would make a statement from Day 1 and I was warning him not to use it as it may follow Murphy's law of "What can go wrong, will" as he would say to me and everyone who would care to listen - "If I fail, I would rather go down BIG" and I was always suggesting that "this has a negative connotation and cause a negative impact - it can also become a SFP - Self - Fulfilling Prophecy- God Forbid! "

Finally, after 5 years of struggle, his investors did not see any sign of break even and saw the business sinking. The only Cash cow was the EDP and that was a single person dependent and not considered very safe. They told him to scout for new investors. The Need was about 5-7 Crores into Capex plus about 2 Crores in OpenX/ Working Capital with the number of students still on roll. With the business stage, no VC, PE, Bank was keen and the numbers were not making sense. Foreign Universities bill is still not passed (OUR PESTLE analysis hope) and not having Assets (Land, building, location) any M&A was also difficult.

It was a good person who failed in business for external reasons. We can do a case study on this but as a friend we helped him find an Advisory role in a University matching his status and home expense needs. We could not generate the funds he needed as the sector had generated NPAs for the Banks which were huge and the need for MBAs and others had diminished tremendously.

The sector councils were becoming ineffective and they had also not given him exclusivity and business was non-profitable. It was time to EXIT AT LEAST temporarily.

"Success is most often achieved by those who don't know that failure is inevitable." – Coco Chanel

"We either make ourselves miserable, or we make ourselves strong. The amount of work is the same." – Carlos Castaneda

CHAPTER 7

Social. Woo. Dominant.

"You Dominate in Social Circles"

Startpreneurs - "You Dominate in Social Circles". Let us see the three distinct Strengths that Pull them towards being on their own and get into business.

A key to success in business is networking and Startpreneurs are naturally inclined to be good at this. In terms of success in life, large and varied social circles allow them more opportunities to find success. I learnt networking from the Ecademy platform much before Facebook or LinkedIn had even started. I joined both and Twitter at their inception and being an early adopter got many followers and close friends.

I discuss here three Related yet distinct Strengths of the Startpreneurs and they are their Social Skills, Woo and Dominant Personality.

1. **A social skill is any skill facilitating interaction and communication with others. With Social Skill, they create** rules and relations, communicate, and change in their verbal and nonverbal ways. **They socialize.** The process of learning these **skills** is called socialization.

2. <u>**Woo stands for winning others over**</u>. Startpreneurs enjoy the challenge of meeting new people and getting them to like them. They do not feel intimidated by Strangers and feel interactions with them energizing. They are drawn to them and want to know their names, ask them questions, and find area of common interest so that you can strike up a conversation and build rapport. Startpreneurs initiate with strangers as they love breaking the ice and making a connection. Once the connection is done they are happy to wrap up and move on. Not only are you rarely at a loss for words; you enjoy initiating with

strangers because you derive satisfaction from breaking the ice and making a connection

3. Startpreneurs have an overt/ under-stated or latent Dominant Personality.

General characteristics of the D Personality Style tends to make them be direct and decisive, sometimes described as dominant. They prefer to lead than follow, and tend to display leadership and managerial tendencies. They have high self-confidence and are risk takers and problem solvers, others to look up to them for decisions and direction. They tend to be self-starters.

"If you don/t have any shadows, you're not standing in the light." - Lady Gaga

CHAPTER 8

Positive. Can Do. Attitude.

Startpreneurs have a Can-Do Attitude

You can handle anything that is thrown your way. New tasks are easily tackled and, because you're you, they are completed with poise. And, it is said that if You Don't Prioritize Your Life, Someone Else Will. A Startpreneur learns early in his/ her life to say YES and to say NO at the appropriate time and place. While the Attitude is still CAN DO - the reasoning to say Yes or No is very logical and sound. It is Priority Driven.

"A 'no' uttered from the deepest conviction is better than a 'yes' merely uttered to please, or worse, to avoid trouble." So, said Mahatma Gandhi, and we all know how his conviction played out on the world stage. But what is less well known is how this same discipline played out privately with his own grandson.

He grew up in South Africa. When he was a young boy, he was beaten up twice: once for being too white and once for being too black. Still angry, Arun was sent to spend time with his grandfather. In an interview with Arun, he said that his grandfather was in demand from many important people, yet he still prioritized his grandson, spending an hour a day for 18 months just listening to him. It proved to be a turning point in Arun's life. He had the opportunity to apply Gandhi's example of prioritization to his own life, hours before one of his daughters was born. He felt pressure to go to a client meeting the next day. But on this occasion, he knew what to do. It was clearly a time to be there for his wife and child. So, when asked to attend the meeting, he said with all the conviction he could muster...f

"Yes."

Read in his own words a real-life story as it was told by someone close:

Quote "To my shame, while my wife lay in the hospital with my hours-old baby, I went to the meeting. Afterward, my manager said, "The client will respect you for making the decision to be here." But the look on the clients' faces mirrored how I felt. What was I doing there?! I had not lived true to Gandhi's saying. I had said "yes" to please.

As it turned out, exactly nothing came of the client meeting. And even if the client had respected my choice, and key business opportunities had resulted, I would still have struck a fool's bargain. My wife supported me and trusted me to make the right choice under the circumstances, and I had opted to de-prioritize her and my child.

Why did I do it? I have two confessions:

First, I allowed social awkwardness to trump making the right decision. I wasn't forced to attend the meeting. Instead, I was so anxious to please that even awkward silent pauses on the phone were too much for me. To stop the social pain, I said "yes" when I knew the answer should be "no."

Second, I believed that "I had to make this work." Logically, I knew I had a choice, but emotionally, I felt that I had no choice. That one corrupted assumption psychologically removed many of the actual choices available to me."end Quote

What can you as Startpreneur do to avoid the mistake of saying "yes" when you know the answer should be "no"? Don't say No when you mean to say Yes or Vice Versa and for God's sake don't mumble say it firmly.

First, we as Startpreneurs must learn to separate the decision from the relationship. Sometimes these seem so interconnected, we forget there are two different questions we need to answer. By deliberately dividing these questions, we can make a more conscious choice. Answer the question, "What is the right decision?" and then "How can I communicate this as kindly as possible?"

Second, we must watch our language. Every time we say, "I must and I must take this call" or "I must send this piece of work off" or "I must go to and I must go to client meeting," we are if previous commitments are non-negotiable. Every time we use the phrase "I must" over the next week, stop and replace it with "I choose to." It can feel a little odd at first — and in some cases, it can even be gut-wrenching (if we are choosing the wrong priority). But ultimately, using this language reminds us that we are making choices, which enables us to make a different choice. While one of my Gurus and Executive Coaches corrected me by making me avoid NEVER and ALWAYS from my sentences - one of them was very stern and told me to make DEFINITE statements and avoid - may be, perhaps and excuses couched behind words like but, however etc. It was tough learning yet very essential. (In another Chapter we shall discuss some such Smart terms that I suggest to Startpreneurs, C-Level Mentees and Entrepreneurs to avoid).

Third, avoid working for or with people who don't respect our priorities. It may sound simplistic, but this is a truly liberating rule! There are people who share our values and thus make it natural to live our priorities. It may take a while to find an employment situation like this, but we can set our course to that destination immediately.

Saying "yes" when we should be saying "no" can seem like a small thing in the moment. But over time, such compromises can create a life of regrets. Indeed, in an Australian nurses' story, who cared for people in the last 12 weeks of their lives, recorded the most often-discussed regrets. At the top of the list: "I wish I'd had the courage to live a life true to myself, not the life others expected of me."

Having worked with the Dutch MNC gave me some opportunity to learn cross cultures. When I presented a Bouquet of her favorite Tulips to my lady boss when I met first time in Amsterdam, she refused to accept them - plainly explaining to me that she does not have a Vase to keep them at home!! May sound naive but it was true and said honestly. I persisted and offered to present her a Vase and then she agreed to accept. Dutch are direct people, they rarely beat around the bush, play diplomatic. They can be brutally honest too. I have made many friends there and I like their honesty. I have a vision of people everywhere having the courage to live a life true to themselves instead of the life others expect of them. As poet Mary Oliver wrote: "Tell me, what is it you plan to do with your one wild and precious life?" I believe to harness the courage we need to get on the right path, it pays to reflect on how short the life is and we have so little time left to accomplish.

Deal with life with a CAN DO, positive Attitude. That is a Key for Startpreneurs's success.

"Life is not easy for any of us. But what of that? We must have perseverance and above all confidence in ourselves. We must believe that we are gifted for something and that this thing must be attained." - Marie Curie

CHAPTER 9

Ambitious Startpreneur

Why Governments are insensitive to Social Entrepreneurship?

Startpreneurs are Ambitious!

There is not much worth to being enterprising if you don't have the ambition to make progress. Your alpha personality makes you want to do more in every aspect of life. "All you need is ignorance and confidence and the success is sure." – Mark Twain saying may sound to have been said in jest yet it is useful.

I support NGOs, Section 8 (Old Sec 25) companies, Trusts in their formation strategy onward as Pro-Bono Advisor. As I retired in early 2012, Walking in the morning and evening became a daily routine. Later, post my cardiac issues and diabetes - it became part of the medical management prescribed.

I now walk between 10-12 Km and keep fit. While walking, I use several trial Health Related Apps to keep testing as an amateur beta tester on my mobile phones. While music and FM Radio Apps are my constant companions - I am fortunate I still watch a lot and it helps me observe things.

I met in Gujarat my friends who are doing pioneering work in Social entrepreneurship using CSR funds which remain un-utilized by the corporates for Skills development and helping Startpreneurs - Micro ones - those who can start business with a Seed capital given as a grant of Rs. 25-40000. That is very small indeed.

On my way of this walk, I visit a Ganapati Temple with a 60Ft tall statue. It is close to a bus-stand and a new Sky-way has come up near the Walkers/ Joggers garden nearby. I have observed recently under the Swachh Bharat program the Municipal corporation has also made a Public Pay toilet on a

BOLT (Build- Own - Lease- Transfer) basis and a family maintains it and keeps it clean and hygienic. This suburb is Bangalore's largest upcoming suburb and at last count there are about Half a Million people live here most of whom get water by tankers as civic amenities are still non-existent.

I was happy to see this initiative of the Pay Toilet which to me is a nice gesture to make a family entrepreneur and self-sufficient while keeping the area clean. In Bangalore city, the Gardens are well maintained but the Gardeners are not well taken care of. They still live in Tent like huts made of gunny sacks and a whole family of 6-10 people lives in the garden - they still cook on wood. The poor gardener also begs and seeks money from morning walkers which is sad.

I see another beggar near the temple and his geographic area seems to be demarcated to Temple, couple of hotels, bus stand and the unauthorized bike parking space. Bangalore is a different type of city. The Politicians here do not care if the pedestrians have footpath or not and bike riders consider it to park on footpaths available as their birthright.

I was thinking of a BOLT, Social entrepreneurship and beggary together. As an Edward, De Bono Lateral thinking follower, I got thinking. I felt why not convert some of the open land under the skywalk, near the garden and outside of the footpath as Paid Parking space with a Manned Parking Meter and allow this beggar and gardener cum beggar to allow it to run on BOLT basis.

What will it entail:

1. Permission from Municipal corporation to convert the empty land and build a compound, fencing around it.

2. Have No Parking boards put up at the designated places in consultation with the Traffic Police.

3. Get a Parking meter and fix the parking rates for the hour, 4 hours, 6 hours, Overnight parking etc. as I have seen people parking for longer durations here.

4. Issue Bar cards to monthly payment users and equip the two-people manning it with Card swipe machines and train them into the usage and help them with a bank account where the bank person comes and collects the cash and charge slips from them and issues a passbook update.

5. I think this can help regulate the traffic in this area, help two families to have sustainable income and over a period the Municipal corporation can

recover its initial investment in fencing, boards, parking meter, printing paper, electricity, no parking boards, swipe machines and training.

I just wish and hope that I am someday able to either get hold of the Corporate to do this or get an influential NGO to influence him, Corporation and provide them the seed capital to run this and get the right permissions.

I sincerely feel that beggary in the town can be regulated and by right parking habits the traffic menace can also be controlled. We see many Third Gender people crowing or knocking the car windows on the Traffic signals demanding money and people mistreating them and getting into fights. This menace can also be curbed if a sympathetic view is taken towards and the business help provided.

CHAPTER 10

Startpreneurs are Competitive

Competitiveness is in the DNA!

THE Startpreneur is Competitive. As Startpreneur we turn everything into a competition. And we must come out the winner. We turn our ambition for success in business and life into a competition and we BELIEVE TO surely end up on top.

The Startpreneurs must try and find answers to some of the following questions:

- What is market concentration for their products/ services?
- What is the Background of the Competitors (traditional, foreign, lots of new players) usually, the information in public domain.?
- How is your product / service Positioned from the Value Chain perspective?
- How have the competitors evolved over the years?
- How are competitors' financials (if available in public domain)?
- How easy you think it will be to grow market share? Any Growth hackers on team with Killer plans?
- How difficult or easy to enter your business sector?
- Who are likely to be your major suppliers and buyers and what power they assert on Strartpreneurs/ Market?
- What Key Industry trends you have seen so far- Good, Bad, Ugly?

- Why in your observation the Industry Growth or Decline important to you?

Some of the recommended frameworks to assess competition are:

1. Porter's Five Forces
2. Industry Lifecycle Analysis
3. Strategic Groups Analysis

A. Using Porter's Five Forces:

Michael Porter's Five Forces analysis provides a framework for the structure analysis of an industry or a market. Porter assumes that competition in an industry depends on five basic forces:

1. Potential New Entrants
2. Internal Rivalry
3. Suppliers
4. Buyers
5. Substitutes (and Complements)

The strength of each force for an industry is identified by considering important technical and economic characteristics. The collective strength of these forces determines the ultimate profit potential and allocation in the industry.

B. Industry Lifecycle Overview

Lifecycle Analysis presumes that sales and profitability in an industry follow a predictable pattern. In this model, we distinguish among five stages of development

1. Introduction

2. . Growth

3. . Maturity

4. . Saturation

5. . Decline/termination

These help us Focus on building customer loyalty and repeat purchases take decisions to Invest in process improvement to reduce manufacturing costs faster than prices are falling and/ or Proactively invest in capacity to maintain cost advantage and discourage additional competitive entry.

The results of Industry Lifecycle Analysis can drive several strategic hypotheses, such as:
- Forecasts of industry or product sales
- Estimations of competitors' strategic moves
- Identification of the appropriate pricing for a product

C. Strategic Groups Analysis

Lastly, we look at Strategic Groups Analysis. The idea behind this framework is that companies that share similar strategies compete more directly with each other than with other firms in the same industry. They are conceptual clusters, as strategic groups are identified merely for analytical purposes to better understand competition within an industry. An industry could have one strategic group if all the firms followed the same strategy, alternatively, each firm in an industry could be in its own strategic group. Identifying strategic groups may help focus analysis on more direct competitors. Startpreneur may not themselves be equipped to do these and here the need arises for having:

Consultant

Advisor.

(In one of the previous volume we have shared with you the distinction between a Consultant/ Advisor and a Mentor).

CHAPTER 11

Self-Control. Startpreneur

Only YOU can Control YOU

"A moderate level of self-control is essential for a startup intention to develop into concrete activity. The higher the level of self-control, the more likely it is for a person intending to become an entrepreneur to put their money where their mouth is."

Self-Control is an Alpha trait that may not be perceived as well by others as your charm, charisma and social popularity. Taking control of your tendencies of a bossy, non-supportive nature, if curbed can guarantee ultimate success. Startpreneurs with a high level of self-control are more likely to get their business idea off the ground.

Self-control is an important factor contributing to taking entrepreneurial action. A moderate level of self-control is essential for a start-up intention to develop into concrete activity.

The higher the level of self-control, the more likely it is for a person intending to become an entrepreneur to put their money where their mouth is.

A further benefit of a moderate to high level of self-control is that such people are less likely to experience emotional states that hinder entrepreneurial behavior.

Beware of three emotional states: doubt, fear and aversion towards certain activities that may be encountered when becoming a Startpreneur.

It is said that, People who can't manage their own lives don't make good entrepreneurs. Small businesses require multi-tasking, work prioritization, and decision-making, with no entourage of assistants and specialists.

That's why Fortune 500 executives usually don't survive as startup CEOs or Startpreneurs. The points below represent the real problem for Startpreneurs trying to manage a startup:

1. Feeling sub-merged and restricted.
2. Initiative to start many things, but showing low Initiative.
3. Deferment and Procrastination. It would help if Startpreneur adopts "do it now" approach and take the to-do lists and priorities rather than in a Crisis order.
4. Thinking too much and having self-doubt, wastes our creative energy.
5. Getting gripped suddenly by fear of failure. Real entrepreneurs look at new opportunities as an exciting and new-life experience. They are energized by the risk, and learn from every failure.
6. Focus on Weakness in the fond hope of becoming strongest in your weakest spot rather than on Strengths and capitalizing/ monetizing them.
7. Running low on confidence and enthusiasm. Self-confidence is key to success
8. Feeling lonely and need to learn and experience the joys of networking, staying informed, delegating and contributing together as a team without dominating.
9. Behaving like a control freak. Learning the Art of delegation and joys of being spontaneous.
10. Managing self is the best preparation for managing a new business.

The ability to maintain control means that emotions are less likely to cloud our judgement, as doubt, fear and aversion are common feelings that can come into play when building an enterprise.

CHAPTER 12

The Refugee Entrepreneur

Who Loved Cricket

In the early 90's I was posted in the Capital as Regional Profit Centre Head and had to visit Punjab which was part of my region. I am Cantonment city we had a small branch with about 10 people. 6 of them were Couriers doing daily pick-ups and deliveries of consignments and some of them on rotation were traveling by train in the night to Capital city with all the consignments (called Load) by Train/ Bus and were called On Train Couriers. It was a high winter when I visited this branch and the city and met the warm staff.

R was a courier. He told me his background. He was from Jammu and during the height of militancy they were displaced and settled in this town by the Army as Refugees and were given space in the Camps. Later they got lands and grants to build Puce houses on small plots on ownership basis. Many like him had to leave school/ college and had to find work. Having lost all their wealth and riches, they were open to do menial jobs involving hard long hours including travel in crowded trains with heavy bags for company.

Couple of years later, I left the company and joined a small outfit in the same business and R came and met me. He said, he has also left the company as the Manager abused and ill-treated him. He said, he has few customers who are willing to give him courier business and he was looking for a Consolidator who can guarantee deliveries at competitive prices. We began dealing with him. His customers were primarily Sports goods manufactures making Hockey's, Cricket bats, Accessories and Players' Gear/ Kit bags etc. and they were sent as samples to all Hockey and cricket playing nations to players and associations. They needed timely delivery, Proof of delivery and competitive pricing. They also needed Secrecy and tight control over the samples which were prototypes and did not want their local competitors to know the addresses or the products they were pitching for.

R was Trusted by them and they were quite benevolent towards him as he would help them with packaging, invoicing and any odd jobs while the packages were getting ready. His simplicity and naiveté was his strong point apart from his reliability, hard work and a broad smile.

Slowly his business flourished. Even as a business owner he would take the night train with Load and come to connect it with us as consolidators by rotation as he had employed 3-4 couriers but being not well literate he still did not have any office staff, sales people, accountant as overheads - he operated business from his small dwellings in the Refugee camp

A hard-working person, he slowly found ways in compliance by hiring Chartered Accountant to manage the books, pay taxes, meet compliance requirements and one lady staff to answer customer queries who also was from his parent state and in need of job.

After couple of years, he opened another branch in another town with the help of Refugees like him in another town which was famous for Hosiery goods, Clothing and Agricultural equipment, Auto parts and was a big wholesale market which had big requirement for domestic courier serving the entire country. He took franchise of a Domestic courier company and expanded business. Within a year he opened three more branches in the major towns of the Northern Indian State and managed he business well.

His key was good relations, good customer service, openly admitting failures without hiding and paying out claims, choice of right consolidators and right pricing. Business flourished.

Recently, he invited me to FB to add as friend and I found that he is now well versed in English, he is married, has children and the invitation to add me was with a reason! His daughter was getting married and he wanted to invite me. I called him after many years! He now own houses in 3 cities, has couple of cars, is well respected in his refugee community and the business community which he serves.

In 1997, I had appointed him a consolidator for TNT and as a goodwill gesture he sent us a full Cricket kit for the entire team and did not accept any money. The TNT cricket team played with local players some of whom made it to the National Team. He continued to supply us the Best of Kashmir Willow Cricket bats which the Stars of Indian Cricket subscribed at very decent rates as well as the cricket kits. These would follow with a huge box full of Cricket Gear / accessories for which he would never accept any payment.

I remember, in 1997 our Global Chairman sent a Scout Manager to Pakistan and India on a Route study. He felt if there could be movement of Logistics Cargo thru the border - it would reduce costs and time of transit. This Manager first visited Lahore and met the special artisans who made Hockey sticks. Post partition the whole families of these artisans shifted to Pakistan taking their special skills with them. India had exporters with Kashmir Willow and other quality wood being produced in India. Being a Dutchman he was well received in both countries and he was received at Indo-Pak Border by Indian exporters and given a warm send off by Pakistani exporters of sports goods. This was a Project for Slazenger of Australia who had suppliers in both countries.

R went and personally met each exporter, arranged the reception at border, took care of Logistics, arranged a grand party (which TNT and the exporters paid for) and it was a gala evening. Exporters praised R to the visitor and said he's the face-of TNT in their town and they love him.

He is grown big but what is not gone is his simplicity, naïveté and the hardworking nature apart from his famous smiling face.

This is a success story of a semi-literate Courier who made it big and who has a GIVING heart when it comes to Cricket and colleagues.

CHAPTER 13

Fired Salesman who bought two Mercedes Cars

Mid-Career Crisis turned around

I met him when we're doing a Fast-Track program of Recruitment of people as we were launching a new Division and needed people at all levels. With his varied experience and job-hoppers' CV - he was shortlisted but not recommended. The guy impressed me with his gift of gab, persuasive, aggressive spiel and varied experience of different industries and interior districts of the State where he was to help us appoint Agents and Franchisees. I took a chance.

Nearly a year later, I met his during a Sales Review and watched the presentation - the numbers were pathetic and practically no targets were being achieved. The Sales Manager was quite unhappy. I called him for counseling and held a detailed One on One Review on all aspects of business development, competition, pricing and his support needs for achieving goals. It worked for couple of quarters the business showed an up-trend and later as it dropped continually and touched a new low the Sales manager decided to fire him. He met me for an Exit interview. He had an acquired Military habit of saying 'Roger Sir! 'which I found amusing and as he always showed allegiance - I asked his future. He had none. Family was a reputed one with his late father being a reputed judge and brothers well placed in government.

I like to focus on people's Strengths and recounted his strengths to him as I saw them and said you network well, you build good relations, have persuasive and aggressive sales pitch, you talk well - you are an Engineer - why not go into a business for yourself. You can even become Company Franchisee.

Few months later, I heard he had started a small workshop and was supplying to a MNC manufacturer in his town as he knew the Purchase manager well and could provide them what they wanted.

I lost touch as I moved town and 5 years later, out of the blue he called. He said he is well settled and doing well. On a hunch, I asked him how is his Mercedes Car? And he said CARS! Sir! (I had read that Mercedes opened a new dealership in his town a year ago and sold 100 Cars on a single day). No kidding - he said I bought two in that lot of 100 Cars. I was Happy and astonished. I said, I am inviting you to my laughers' marriage - come in the Merc and show me around. He came and like he always did when I was alone in my cabin - touched my feet and asked for blessings. I congratulated him.

I asked how did he find the Key to success. He said, for the past 5 years it is with one sole client the MNC for whom he supplies parts as per their specifications and due to his past engineering knowledge - manages Quality well. The pricing was favorable; he knew where to source cheaper material at JIT terms with good credit and business is profitable. I asked him whether initial funding was difficult? He said yes, first couple of months were tough but he knew a Banker / Manager who offered him to Discount /Factor his bills initially and as the payment cycle was good with the MNC reputation - he was offered Overdraft and Cash Credit (against stocks) limit. He did not splurge the money but invested wisely in paying off the debt on home loan/ bought the Shed in which he was producing and found a way to buy a good property of a BIFR case (Loan defaulter company which was under Bureau of Industrial Financial Reconstruction). Along the way, an offer was made by the Dealer to buy Mercedes car on easy EMI and very low interest. He found that his MNC Principal needed two Mercs on Rent for their Expat Senior officials at a very good rent provided he could provide a trained Chauffeur with each car. So, our man as a true salesman made a good back-to-back deal with the company and the dealer and bought two cars!

Of course, this brought him some trouble with the Income Tax authorities but he paid all taxes on time and had hired good chartered accountant who could explain to the tax authorities and was at Peace.

I felt very happy for him and complimented and thanked him for coming over for the marriage ceremony. Today, he does not own Merc but has 3 Cars and two bungalows and loves driving across the country with family on holidays rather than using Train or Flight. I had suggested to him that Single Pillar Circus or dependence on Sole customer is not wise and he must find ways to enhance his portfolio to few good customers - he accepted the advice with his customary "Roger Sir!" And sought blessings. He now has diverse range of customers for whom he supports in engineering design and custom makes the parts with Quality and has a record of delivering on time.

A Success Story of a man who had a mid-career crisis but bootstrapped well, tightened his belt and worked hard to make this possible.

CHAPTER 14

The Taxi Or not to AIR(Port) Taxi

Chapter Number 14
The Taxi Or AIR(Port) Taxi
MY Risk-Taker Ex-Driver

City of Bengaluru. My worst struggles in past decade since I chose this town as my Retirement abode was finding Drivers, Retaining them. While in the Corporate job, there were more people to help but as I retired the woes became higher. I would have, (counting) hired, fired, tried to retain and have one at present at least 25 drivers to date.

Many of them I do not even remembers by name, face also and as I have changed my mobiles at $1/4_{th}$ the frequency of changing drivers - this time moving from Apple to Android phone - I lost all their mobile numbers too. So, it is a difficult memory :)

I do remember two of them though and for good reason. One guy was from Pondicherry and he was with me for the longest duration i.e. 3 years! And now has his part-owned truck which he drives himself on a NP - National Permit - mostly to Mumbai. Sometimes he feels like calling me and while passing Bengaluru he gives me a call just to say his regards and asks about family members etc. It is a very good conversation I like and when he is in town - usually, we offer him snacks, tea, coffee, lunch depending upon the time of his visit and give him some gift. He loves it. I like that he is on his own now - has paid off the loan on his village house, regained control of the jewelry pawned by his father for his own treatment and is jolly as ever. He recounts the trips we took together to nearby places in Bengaluru, Iupati, Chennai, Pondicherry etc. He was a flawless driver and had excellent command over the steering and had a cool temperament and had learnt as an ex-truck driver to shun eyes and ears towards Road rage makers. I liked his safe driving and would use him with our company drivers on Defensive driving classroom trainings.

The Second one I remember is because even though he is not in my employment - he is available 24x7 to us if he is in town and always treats us with 1st Priority. He was just 20 when he joined me. A Village boy who know driving, had worked for a travel taxi company for a short while and was finding his feet in the Bengaluru town.

After working with me for nearly 3 years he once came to me and said he is planning to quit and become an AIRPORT taxi driver with an aggregator. He showed the economics and shared his family commitments and responsibilities and convinced me with his sound logic. I let him go. I asked him if I needed a Cab and called him - will he provide me the service. He said he would be more than will in to do.

He is a successful cab owner today and he knows that Every ride is custom. People choose a cab precisely because they can ride alone, on their own terms without much disturbance - speaking over phone, listening to music, working on Laptops/ tabs or simply asking the Cab driver to play local FM Radio channel music.

He tells me that empty trips are part of the job, and it's okay, because the next ride will pay for it. He is ever willing to accept my request to come 24X7 and usually as I take early morning flights - he comes early and sleeps in the car or comes early at 2 AM and joins me in the morning Copa Tea/ Coffee before we both take the ride to Airport. Family is used to him and like his quiet demeanor which they feel is very respectful. Over past 5 years he changed 3 Taxi Aggregators and now has his own Cab with bank loan. His sister is married, he and his elder brother are engaged - his would be Wife has a job in Bengaluru - the house in his hometown that he regularly visits is now well done up both externally and internally and his parents are happy.

Achieving this was not easy. He worked 18-20 hours a day for first 2 years clearly CHASING money - the only rest period being the visits to the village or festivals and holidays. This worked well for him and he saved money for the Margin money for the car loan from the bank.

While he knows each trip for him is custom made for the traveler/ passenger; on the other hand, the person who chooses to run an Airline knows: that every flight route is designed by me, and people sign up precisely because I planned Route/ Timing well. People choose an airline flight to be with other people, to benefit from economies of scale and to be part of something. For both - the Airport Taxi Driver or an Air Taxi Operator Empty trips (or worse, half-empty trips) can put the airline or Taxi driver out of business. It's easy to get into the cab business. Do a few rides for friends, then list online, or join shared taxi, then go full-time. On the other hand, it's much more difficult to get into the Air Taxi or full-fledged Airline business. There's a critical mass, and the minimum numbers you require are a lot more than one customer.

Each business can be a good one if you do it at the appropriate scale. My ex-Driver knew it well. For the first car, which was a Mahindra Logan - he did 3,00,000Km before switching to another operator who gave him a new car to drive - it was another Mahindra - a Verity this time and he again did 3,00,000 Km and was happy about consumption of diesel and maintenance charges. When he bought his first with Uber - it was a Toyota and he did not like the body which he said is not quite tough, the balance at 80km/hr. not very good and finally switched to a Marti Swift Dire (a Sedan with boot space for passenger luggage). He says, it drives well, is a tough car and gives a great mileage with low maintenance.

The warning, and the purpose of the metaphor, is to realize that it's not a matter of gradually going from one to the other. Remembering that running a taxi is a fine sort of business, but don't expect to turn it into an Air Taxi. And vice versa.

My last business partner was the first Private Air Taxi Operator registered in the country flying fixed winged aircrafts. His specialty was Helicopters - especially the ones required by Oil companies to go to their Platforms in the High Seas. They struggled to keep the Airline afloat - made huge losses and came out.

The Key question people ask when buying a scooter, motor bike, car, truck or bus is "KITNA DEGI" i.e. What is the Per liter Mileage this vehicle will give and followed by whether it runs on Petrol, Diesel, CNG etc. The Air Taxi Operator gets options of Dry or Wet leases but being unsure of the traffic and route productivity often make mistakes in choice of the Aircraft which go semi-filled or Empty at times making operations unviable. In India, the failure rate of Air Taxi operators, Cheap airlines and even full service airlines is not enviable. In comparison - the Taxi business soon takes off.

I met a Taxi operator in Ahmedabad recently and he said - My car gives me a Per Km cost of INR 3.5 while the Aggregators charge 12 to 20 INR per Kilometers - Drivers don't make money with them - the aggregators with their financing schemes, EMI and commissions for managing the booking and navigational system, Billings do not let the drivers become rich and as this key stakeholder suffers - a Driver for them will be a rare resource going forward. You do not need to listen to any Management Expert once you have heard this Voice of Dissent from the Core Stakeholder in the business.

CHAPTER 15

Quick Statistics on Indian Entrepreneurs and Indian Startups

Chapter Number 15

Quick Statistics on Indian Entrepreneurs and Indian Startups

I am sharing below recently published Business Today article featuring India's Hottest Startups.

The article lists startups from many different industries, from organic food to technology. Below are the following points I observed/calculated from the article:

- Average age of a founder is 37.
- Standard deviation in the age of founders is 8.
- Youngest entrepreneur is 26 and the oldest one is 58. Wow, what a difference!
- Average amount of funding: Rs. 25 crores. (USD 6.25 million)
- Range of funding: Rs 0 - Rs 72 crore. (USD 18 million)
- Average amount of revenues: 25.2 crore (USD 6.25 million). Surprise! Notice how much the average funding and average revenues match.
- Range of revenues: Rs 0 - Rs 110 crore. (USD 27.5 million)

The Climate is HOT for Entrepreneurship. Under the Ease of Doing Business, 1200 archaic rules coming in the way of business have been done away with.

CHAPTER 16

Best Business Climate for Startpreneurs in India

n India, best period has come for new business and entrepreneurship is now at an all-time high

Prime Minister Narendra Modi, Finance Minister Arun Jaitley and Minister of States for Independent Charge Nirmala Sitharaman released the Action Plan at the launch of Start-Up India at Vigyan Bhavan on January 16, 2016.

India is witnessing the major growth trend - entrepreneurship — A bug called BOOM - Being One's Own man/woman and that is the main reason rather than chasing Employability skills and chasing jobs via applications and interviews. In IT sector the job security is becoming non-existent as USA tightened the H1B VISA rules and many MBAs who were on the 'Bench Strength' and many seniors are finding it difficult to get re-employed. Re-skilling, Re-tooling are just jargons flying which are not helping this crop of youngsters.

With 65 percent of population under 35 years of age and a record-breaking growth in smartphone adoption and data services/ digital banking, Payment Banks, e-Commerce across the country, there is a rise in demand for next-gen services that offer simplified solutions.

While India sees this exponentially growing trajectory of entrepreneurs and new start-ups over the last five years, 2016 was a major milestone year for all of the key stakeholders in the Indian ecosystem that included government, Academic institutions, entrepreneurship support organizations, Venture capitalists, Angel investors, Private equity, Accelerators, Incubation centers by Industry departments and Universities and entrepreneurs themselves— to seek and provide support in sustaining the biggest hurricane of entrepreneurship to date.

Major factors which fueled the momentum

"Startup India" action plan to provided entrepreneurs with various subsidies, as well as relaxed norms for starting up businesses in India.

The government of India's Innovation arm, Nitti Aayog — the National Institution for Transforming India —announced there will be up to $2 million in support for those setting up and modernizing existing start-up incubators across the country — as well as to promote entrepreneurship right at the high school level. The growth in demand from entrepreneurs seeking support through mentorship, capital assistance, legal advice and more to ensure the sustainability of their ventures is on the rise.

From students and women entrepreneurs to policymakers and investors, we see everyone celebrate entrepreneurship, share their own entrepreneurial journeys and provide support to keep this momentum going.

With the newly launched Digital India initiative by the government of India, we notice a huge increase in tech start-ups and mobile applications. This is due to the adoption of digital practices.

CHAPTER 17

Successful Indian Entrepreneurs

Chapter Number 16
New Age Successful Indian Entrepreneurs
They Are Just Brilliant

The new Wave of Entrepreneurship - will it be India's Game changer? Only time will tell. Celebrating success by sharing the very inspiring short success stories of First Generation Entrepreneurs overwhelms India as these young Men and Women not only create Wealth - they also helped create Employment for Indian job seekers. We laud here their out of the box thinking, leadership qualities and unique styles of execution.

We are sharing some of the stories - they are in public domain but can certainly help the new generation of Startpreneurs as Icons/ Idols and some of them help in Mentoring the Startpreneurs.

SACHIN BANSAL & BINNY BANSAL (FLIPKART) - A True UNICORN.

Year 2007, Month October - Sachem Bansal and Binny Bansal launch an e-commerce website retailing books. Today, the near-20% stake they hold, along with the top management and company is valued at around US$16Bn. (source: CB insights) They initially spend (Skin in the game = as the jargonizes would call it) 400,000 only for making website to set up the business.

VIJAY SHEKHAR SHARMA (PAYTM)

Born in Aligarh, UP in a modest family Vijay Shephard Sharma is an startpreneur and founder of Paytm. Paytm's current value is a little over $3 billion in the market in 2016. He dreamt a dream when it was struggling to make both ends meet with just Rs. 10 in his pocket, he has tasted Victory and Paytm is now also a Payment Bank recognized by the RBI. It did not come easy. He has also given 4% of his equity to the team members, which is currently valued at $120 million.

NAVEEN TEWARI (INMOBI)

He has a Bachelor's degree in Mechanical Engineering from Indian Institute of Technology, Kanpur (IIT) from where he passed out in 2000. He is the Founder and CEO of InMobi. It is a Leader in global mobile advertising and technology platform. He is also a Board member of Paytm. Simply put, InMobi competes against Google's AdMob Millennial media and Apple's iAd.

Naveen has motivated and is personally involved with fuelling of 30 start-ups in India and not just by investments alone, he is a a mentor and support to several start-ups like NestAway, Slide Rule, Mettle, Money sights, Bombay Canteen, Zimmber, Razor pay etc. Naveen co-founded iSPIRT, a change agent with the brain of a think tank and aims to address government policy, create market catalysts, and grow the maturity of product entrepreneurs to transform India into a hub for new generation software products.

ALOK KEJRIWAL

Alok Kejriwal the CEO and Co-Founder of Games2Win.com; apart from being a serial entrepreneur and investor, he is also a very active individual in the Indian startup ecosystem. His aim to fame came when he Sold his last Company to Walt Disney. Games2win is among global top 20 online games business entertaining over 20 million unique users a month. The top games include Parking Frenzy (also ranked #1 on the US iTunes Appstore.

KUNAL BEHL & ROHIT BANSAL (SNAPDEAL)

They just spurned the offer to buy for $950 Million made by FLIPKART and its investors and made waves in the media. The SnapDeal 2.0 is readying for a makeover launch. Started in 2010, by Kunal Bahl and Rohit Bansal got bitten by the BOOM bug they chose, offline coupons business and named it MoneySaver. Snapdeal went online in 2010. It is estimated that currently, it has over 200,000 sellers which sell around 15 million+ products on Snapdeal.

BHAVISH AGGARWAL (OLA CABS)

Ola was valued at $5 billion as of September 2015. Chaseing his dream of entrepreneurship, Bhavish started an online holiday and tour planning service, before changing it into OlaCabs on 3 December 2010. On that day. Bhavish Aggarwal (currently CEO) and Ankit Bhati founded the company. Bhavish did B. Tech in Computer Science from IIT, Bombay. Worked in Microsoft Research, Bangalore for 2 years, right after college.

DHIRAJ RAJARAM (MU SIGMA)

Dhiraj Rajaram founded and is Chairman of Mu Sigma Inc. It is a data analytics company- Mu Sigma Inc. Founded in 2004. Mu Sigma is valued over 1 Billion and headquartered in Chicago with its main delivery centre in Bangalore.

SHASHANK ND (PRACTO)

Shashank, was a biotechnology student from NIT, Surathkal (Karnataka), before he embarked to build a software to simplify health care. He roped in class buddy Abhinav Lal, 27, and together founded Practo Ray, an online management software that allows doctors to upload and store medical records and prescriptions, patient history, billing schedule, make appointments, etc.

This healthcare app is now being used in 15 countries and over 50 cities across the globe. It has a listing of 200,000 doctors, 10,000 hospitals, 8000 diagnostic centers and over 4000 wellness centers globally and receives over 10M searches a month across its website and apps.

DEEPINDER GOYAL (ZOMATO)

Deepinder who co-founded Zomato, a restaurant search and discovery service with Pankaj Chadda, conceived the idea of an online restaurant information service after observing demand for paper menu cards among his colleagues at Bain, where he worked as a management consultant. Deepinder is a graduate with Integrated Masters in Mathematics and Computing from IIT Delhi in 2005. As on 21th March 2016, Zomato ranks as the top 2 startup for India in the StartupRanking. It currently operates in 23 countries, including India, Australia and the United States.

SAMAR SINGLA (JUGNOO)

Samar Singla is a Founder/ CEO at Jugnoo, a Chandigarh based auto rickshaw aggregator. He also founded Click Labs, a technology solution provider. He worked as a Researcher in University of Maryland. He was a Researcher at IBM & also worked as a Scientist at CERN.

SAURABH KUMAR & ALBINDER DHINDSA (GROFFERS)

Saurabh Kumar & Albinder Dhindsa co-founded Grofers, an on-demand delivery service that connects consumers with local stores. It worked on a B2B model for a few months then started the B2C business to cater end consumers directly. Saurabh is a graduate of IIT Bombay and University of Texas in Austin while Albinder is a graduate of IIT Delhi and holds an MBA from Columbia University.

RITESH AGARWAL (OYO ROOMS)

A well known personality - Ritesh is founder and CEO at OYO Rooms. He was selected for the 20 under 20 Thiel Fellowship which makes him one of the very few Indians shortlisted. He began working early in his life at the age of 13 and by 18 he was building OYO Rooms. Recently, he was named by Forbes in its "30 Under 30" list in the consumer tech sector.

SWATI BHARGAVA (CASHKARO)

Swati Bhargava - a classic Investment Banker turned entrepreneur. She's An alumni of London School of Economics. Swati has worked at Goldman Sachs in London. S She frost started Pouring Pounds with her husband Rohan Bhargava in the UK in 2011. Observing huge opportunity in India they launched Cashkaro.com in April 2013 & it is now India's largest Cash-back & Coupon website.

RADHIKA AGGARWAL (SHOP CLUES)

Radhika Aggarwal is CEO at ShopClues is an online marketplace, headquartered in Gurgaon, India. The company entered the unicorn club earlier this year and currently covers 29,000 plus pin codes across the country and plans to add 5,000 more pin codes this year. ShopClues is believed to be valued at more than $1.1 billion.

These are just some of the BIG Achievers Startpreneurs and the list is huge.

CHAPTER 18

India's Most Successful Women Startpreneurs

Chapter Number 17
India's Most Successful Women Startpreneurs
Sabha Saath Sabha Vikas - Inclusive Growth Mantra

Women Startpreneurs of India - 2016 was an interesting year for the Women Startpreneurs. It was also the best year for all Indian Startups. What's great to see is that many women Entrepreneurs in india have been just as enterprising as their male counterparts and made a name for themselves with their ventures.

As the year ends, let's take a look at some of the best women entrepreneurs who made us sit up and take notice in 2015...

MEET SOME of the most Successful WOMEN Startpreneurs of INDIA

Ms. Padmaja Ruparel Company: Indian Angel Network Age: 45, Education: BA Hons, Loreto House. Prior Work Experience: Xansa India Indian Angel Network is India's first angel investor network. They have gone global by partnering with Inventus Capital Partners to invest in two US-based startups. IAN, which has over 350 members globally, counts prominent angel investors such as Hero Cycles managing director Sunil Munjal, HCL cofounder Ajai Chowdhry and Sanjeev Bikhchandani, cofounder and chief executive of publicly-listed internet company Info Edge, in its network.

Ms. Falguni Nayar Company: nykaa.com Age: 45, Education: IIM Ahmedabad. Prior Work Experience: Temasek, Kotak, The entrepreneurial dream of Falguni Nayar is nykaa.com, She is the former MD Of Kotak Mahindra Capital Company. Recently TVS Capital invested about Rs.25 crore they received Rs.60-crore Series C fundraising are a clutch of investors, including high net-worth individuals, non-resident Indians (NRIs) and family offices

Ms. Ankita Vashistha, Company: Saha Fund, Age: 34, Education: Masters in Finance, Cranfield School of Management, UK, Prior Work Experience: Aureos Capital Ankita Vashistha launched Saha Fund, a venture capital fund for women centric businesses run by women. The Saha Fund, is a prime mover as India's first Securities and Exchange Board of India-approved venture capital fund focused on women entrepreneurs, and would have a corpus of Rs 100 crore. They would invest in companies run by women entrepreneurs as founders or senior management. The fund has investments from Mohandas Pai and Kiran Mazumdar Shaw.

Ms. Pankhuri Shrivastava, Company: Grabhouse, Age: 25, Education: BE Computer Science, Rajiv Gandhi Technolohgy University. Prior Work Experience: Teach For India

Grabhouse is a broker-free website that helps people finding apartments, sharing rooms and PG's on rent. Grabhouse raised $2.5 million from Kalaari Capital and Sequoia Capital. The startup now has more than 1.5 lakh visitors a day.

Ms. Ankita Sheth, Company: Vista Rooms. Age: 32, Education: MET. Prior Work Experience: OYO Rooms, Stanton Chase, Boston Analytics Ankita Sheth is Co-Founder for Vista Rooms, one of India's fastest growing online aggregators for budget hotels. She is also the only women entrepreneur in this highly male dominated segment. Vista Rooms have scaled 700 plus properties in 70 plus locations across India in under six months of their inception. They also command the largest inventory for tier II and tier III locations in India.

Ms. Shivani Siroya. Company: Inventure. Age: 30 . Education: Columbia University. Prior Work Experience: Healthnet InVenture is a mobile technology and data science company that is flipping the traditional credit scoring model by putting power into the hands of newly empowered consumers in emerging markets.They have raised $10 million series A round to launch into additional markets in Sub-Saharan Africa and Asia.

Ms. Vani Kola. Company: Kalaari Capital, Age: 38. Prior Work Experience: Arizona State University. Work: Certus Software, Rightworks Kalaari Capital, a venture capital firm, has invested in more than 25 start ups including Snapdeal, Zivame and Urbanladder. Kalaari Capital has recently launched its third $290M India fund.

Name Swati Bhargava. Company: cashkaro.com. Age: 30. Education: London School Of Economics. Prior Work Experience: Goldman Sachs - Cashkaro.com is touted to be India's largest & fastest growing Cashback & Coupons site. Cashkaro.com is planning its foray into new countries after raising a $3.8 million Series A from Kalaari Capital.

Ms.Mamta Chhikara, Company: Bizztor, Age: 25, Education: MDU Rohtak. Prior Work Experience: Bizztor Connecting Indian Entrepreneurs, startups & SMEs, Indianbizparty is a platform for Latest startup stories, Learning & Networking inIndian Startup eco system.

Ms. Pranshu Bhandari, Company: Culture Alley, Age: 26, Education: Narsee Monjee Institute of Management Studies, Work: Wipro. The startup launched its English language learning Apps in Oct 2014. In eight months the English app has seen 3 million installs on Android from India. They have recently raised $6 million from Tiger Global and Kae Capital.

Ms. Richa Kar, Company: Zivame, Age: 30, Education: Narsee Monjee Institute of Management Studies, Prior Work Experience: SAP, Spencer's Retail Ltd., Zivame is probably the first in online lingerie space in India and has played a role in educating women across the country about intimate wear and shaping consumer behaviour. It has recently raised a Series C round of Rs 250 crore from Zodius Technology Fund and Khazanah Nasional Berhad.

Ms. Shradha Sharma, Company: Yourstory. Age: 30. Prior Work Experience: MICA. Work: CNBC TV18, The Times Of India, YourStory is a portal publishing original stories of entrepreneurs. They have received their first round of funding from marquee investors, Kalaari Capital, Qualcomm Ventures, T V Mohandas Pai and Ratan Tata.

Ms. Upasana Taku, Company: Mobikwik, Age: N/A, Education: Stanford University. Prior Work Experience: Paypal, Zaakpay, 2020 Social. MobiKwik is India's fastest growing mobile wallet trusted by 25 Million users & 50,000 merchants. With 17 M-wallet users, MobiKwik plans to raise $100 M.

Ms. Meena Ganesh, Company: Growth Story. Age: 40. Education: IIM Calcutta. Prior Work Experience: Microsoft India, Tesco. Meena and Ganesh, the founder couple of venture building platform GrowthStory, built and sold four companies over two decades. Growth Story has a corpus of approximately Rs 200 crore. And it already has a portfolio of five e-commerce ventures — BigBasket, BlueStone, Delyver, MustSeeIndia, and BookAdda.

Ms. Rashmi Daga. Company: Freshmenu, Age: 30, Education: IIM Ahmedabad, Prior Work Experience: afday.com Fresh Menu is a company that offers ready-to-eat/heat and serve meal plans. The Bangalore-based Internet-first restaurant, FreshMenu, part of serial entrepreneur K Ganesh's startup factory GrowthStory, is all set to raise INR 31 Cr in a first round of funding from Lightspeed Venture Partners.

Ms. Shuchi Mukherjee Company: LimeRoad Age: 42 Education: London School Of Economics Previous Work Experience: Gumtree, an eBay Inc Company, Skype, eBay Inc Ask any woman today who binges on online shopping and this LimeRoad will definitely pop up. Founder Shuchi Mukherjee comes from a family with no business background and has managed to give biggies like Flipkart and Snapdeal tough competition. A post grad from London School of Economics, Shuchi has worked with companies like eBay, Skype and Gumtree.

Ms. Nidhi Agarwal, Company: Kaaryah, Age: 30, Education: MBA from Kellogg School of Management. Prior Work Experience: Export houses in Delhi. is a brand of western formal wear for Indian women focused on providing the best possible fit with its 18 sizes. The brand focuses on bridging the gap between western formals and the Indian silhouette. Recently Ratan Tata has picked up a minor stake in Kaaryah.

Manisha Raisinghani: Company: LogiNext Age: 27 Education: Masters, MIS, Carnegie Mellon University Prior Work Experience: IBM LogiNext funded by Indian Angel Network is a technology based startup, providing real- time visibility and optimization solutions to logistics companies. LogiNext Solutions had raised its seed round of funding of about $600k from Indian Angel Network in March 2015. This was followed by another funding round in September 2015, wherein it raised a whopping $10 Mn Series A funding from Paytm.

Debadtta Upadhaya Company: Timesaverz Age: 35 Prior Work Experience: IIM Calcutta Work: The Times of India, Yahoo! India and Vdopia Inc Timesaverz is a one-stop solution for home service requirement. It connects customers to home service providers who are certified, verified and curated. The service majorly includes home maintenance and one-time services. Recently Unilazer Ventures invested Rs 15 crores in Timesaverz. '

Anika Tekriwal Company: JetSetGo Age: 27 Prior Work Experience: Coventry University Work: Aviation industry JetSetGo is India's first and only marketplace for private jet and helicopter charters. JetSetGo raised nearly Rs 12.73 crore from Puneet Dalmia and others in 2015 in pre-series A funding.

Neha Motwani Company: Fitternity Age: 30 Education: MMS, Welingkar Institute of Management Prior Work Experience: HSBC, Axis Risk Consulting Fitternity is catering to holistic preventive healthcare space covering exercise (working out), eat (eating right) and explore (mental wellbeing). Fitternity Health E-solutions has raised pre-series A investment of USD 1M led by Bengaluru-based Exfinity Venture Partners.

Namrata Bostrom Company: POPxo Age: 28 Education: MBA, London Business School Prior Work Experience: EBITD, BCG POPxo is a dynamic digital media platform attracting over 3 million loyal and engaged readers every month for go-to fashion, beauty and lifestyle destination for young women across the country. POPxo has raised USD 2 Million in series A funding from IDGVI, Kalaari Capital.

Company: Helper4U Age: 47 Education: JNU Delhi Prior Work Experience: Tata Interactive Systems Helper4U is a Job portal for semi-skilled and unskilled workers looking for jobs as housemaids, cooks, drivers, caretakers, babysitters, housekeeping staff, office boys, courier boys etc. In simple words, Helper4U.in facilitates a direct connect between the Job Seeker and Job Giver to transform the way Bottom of the Pyramid workers find jobs; leveraging the penetration of mobile devices and internet connectivity in India. Helper4U provides Internet-based classified listings of semi-skilled and unskilled workers looking to find a job. In our process, we are doing away with the need of a middleman, and allowing for immediate, more cost effective, direct hiring.

This list, brimming with women Entrepreneurs who've shown unparalleled enthusiasm and dedication towards their work makes me the happiest to say - it's not a man's world after all!

CHAPTER 19

Entrepreneurs Success Stories

Entrepreneurs Success Stories

What should Startpreneur Study?

I am sure many of you would have seen this. I am sharing as I liked this one but I am unable to give credit as to who compiled this list and made into a Quote Meme. Apologies.

- Facebook – COO Sheryl Sandberg studied economics
- YouTube – CEO Susan Wojcicki studied History Literature at Harvard
- Salesforce – Co-Founder Parker Harris studied English at Middlebury
- Alibab – founder Jack Ma was an English teacher
- Snapchat – Former COO Emily White studied Fine and Studio Arts at Vanderbilt
- PayPal – Co-Founder Peter Thiel studied Philosophy and Law
- LinkedIn – Founder Reid Hoffman studied Philosophy at Oxford
- Hewlett Packard – Former CEO Carly Fiorina studied Medieval History
- Pinterest – Founder Ben Silbermann studied Political Science at Yale
- Thumbtack – Co-Founder Jonathan Swanson studied Political Science
- Slack – Founder Stewart Butterfield studied Philosophy undergrad and grad
- Palantir – CEO Alex Karp has a PhD in Neoclassical Social Theory

What was common in them -Startpreneurs' zeal, enthusiasm and a FINISHIATIVE.

CHAPTER 20

Is there any right age for a startup?

STARTPRENEURS At 61 - Gurgaon Couple Setting An Example With Happy Clothing - (names changed)

Faced with a mid-career crisis I started business when I was 40 and by 43, a near bankrupt with 6 huge failures I was in the job market! I started my first business when I was 12! My belief is there is no right age to enter business. Post my retirement, after my health issues which prevented Pro-bono teaching - I indulged in pursuing my childhood hobby of Drawing and Painting for 3 years. Last month, I began writing e-books - Published 5 already on KDP Amazon and Paperbacks on Draft2Digital a at 64 !

I recently came across an inspiring story of Mr. K (Retired Civil Eng from), I am sharing this so as to remove inhibitions from the Executives facing loss of jobs/ mid-career crisis or people who are retired find some inspiration.

Mr. K 63 and his Wife Mrs.K (62) started their venture sukhivastra not for survival but with an intent to get recognition for the skills of Mrs. Rathee (who makes good garments). The have a Daughter/ 2 Sons and both sons are working and married. It was not a pursuit of a dream at this stage of life. When most Retirees sit in the Sun spending Pension money. They named their range as Happy Clothes (Comfort clothes, happy clothes). Hear their story:

1. How did it all start? : What was your motivation to start at this age?

My wife Mrs. K did say to me to start our HappyClothes online business of clothing and as a perfect partner I find this thing very interesting and said yes in first Instant.

2. What really inspired you, Who advised you to start?

None. We inspire each other, only to have something of our interest and challenge ourselves in this E-commerce business we started.

3. What are the main challenges you are facing with your startup?

Trained and hardworking craftsman are in short supply in the market.

4. What are your future plans to scale (grow) your business? We do have ambition to grow like the big players with higher production and sales and growth of business. e.g. Flipkart, Shopclues etc. We hope to achieve this by sticking to our core valises which are : selling a great product, excellent customer service and fulfillment of need of each customer.

5. Who supports you to run day to day activities (like order management, shipping, customer service etc). We started this business :me and my wife. We support each other, we do have an IT consultant.

6. Any advice you want to give to young Startpreneurs (startups):

By Determination, handwork and discipline as good citizens of India we can make India a better place and young entrepreneurs have our best wishes.

Age does not matter for entrepreneurial success? Age, in itself does not matter to forecast entrepreneurial success. Experience does, and often times, it comes with age. Smart entrepreneurs who lack experience, can offset it by surrounding themselves with experienced mentors.

www.ingramcontent.com/pod-product-compliance
Lightning Source LLC
Chambersburg PA
CBHW051049180526
45172CB00002B/567